The Big Bug

by Larry Kelly

Illustrated by Ann Iosa

Target Skill Review

PEARSON

Scott
Foresman

My big bug is a mess.

Can Wes fix it?

"Yes," said Wes, "I can fix it."
"It will be fun to fix a big bug."

It will be fun to fix a big bug.

It will be the best.

Wes will tap it.

He taps the big bug.

Wes will rap on it.

He raps on the big bug.

Wes will mix red and yellow.

Wes will dot it on.

Look at the big bug.

I like my red and yellow big bug.